© 2024 by Aya. All rights reserved. No part of this book may be reproduced, stored in a retrieval system, or transmitted in any form or by any means—electronic, mechanical, photocopying, recording, or otherwise—without prior written permission from the copyright owner, except as permitted by applicable law.

The information contained in this book is based on research and the author's experience and is provided solely for guidance. Every family estate situation is unique, and the strategies discussed may not be suitable or effective in all circumstances. The content is not intended as legal advice or a substitute for the professional services of a qualified probate attorney or living estate attorney. Readers are strongly encouraged to consult with a licensed attorney regarding their specific circumstances before making any decisions related to estate planning or trust administration.

Foreword

To every reader who finds themselves at the helm of a family estate, entrusted with the responsibility of a living trust, I offer my heartfelt encouragement. Managing a family's legacy is both an honor and a challenge, often undertaken during times of change and emotion.

Family Legacy Keeper: Strategies for Managing Family Estates with Grace and Fairness is written to guide you through the complexities of serving as a living trust executor, with empathy, clarity, and practical advice. My hope is that these pages will help you navigate your duties with confidence, protect family relationships, and ensure fairness for all involved.

Wishing you strength, wisdom, and grace as you steward your family's legacy. May this book be a trusted companion on your journey.

Family Legacy Keeper: Strategies for Managing Family Estates with Grace and Fairness. Navigating as a Living Trust Executor.

Contents

Understanding Living Trusts and Executor Responsibilities..........1

Preparing for the Role of Executor..2

Dealing with Grief and Family Dynamics..3

Managing Assets and Finances...4

Communication and Transparency..5

Resolving Disputes and Handling Greed..6

Legal Considerations and Compliance...7

Distribution of Assets and Closing the Estate...............................8

Chapter 1: Understanding Living Trusts and Executor Responsibilities
Explanation of living trusts and their role in estate planning
Duties and responsibilities of an executor in managing a living trust.

Chapter 2: Preparing for the Role of Executor
Steps to take before becoming an executor.
Importance of understanding the terms of the living trust.

Chapter 3: Dealing with Grief and Family Dynamics
Addressing emotional challenges after the loss of parents.
Strategies for handling conflicts among siblings.

Chapter 4: Managing Assets and Finances
Inventorying assets and liabilities of the estate.
Collaborating with financial professionals and legal advisors.

Chapter 5: Communication and Transparency
Importance of clear communication with siblings and beneficiaries.
Strategies for maintaining transparency throughout the process.

Chapter 6: Resolving Disputes and Handling Greed
Identifying signs of greed among siblings.
Techniques for resolving conflicts and preventing disputes.

Chapter 7: Legal Considerations and Compliance
Overview of legal requirements for estate administration.
Ensuring compliance with tax laws and regulations.

Chapter 8: Distribution of Assets and Closing the Estate
Steps involved in distributing assets according to the living trust.
Closing procedures for completing the estate administration process.

Conclusion

These chapters provide a comprehensive guide for executors on managing living trusts, communicating effectively, resolving conflicts, ensuring legal compliance, and successfully distributing assets while upholding family legacies with grace, integrity, and fairness.

Chapter 1: Understanding Living Trusts and Executor Responsibilities

A living trust is a legal document, like a will, outlines how you want your assets managed after your passing. Unlike a will, a living trust can help avoid probate, maintain control of assets during incapacity, and ensure privacy. Probate is the legal process where debts are settled, and assets distributed according to a will or state law if there is no will or living trust established.

Benefits of a Living Trust Over a Will

Avoiding Probate: A living trust bypasses probate, saving time and costs associated with the process. Forming a living trust with a qualified Living Trust Attorney is key to avoiding probate.

Control During Incapacity: With a living trust, you retain control of your assets even if you become incapacitated.

Privacy: Unlike wills, living trusts remain private as they do not go through the probate process.

Executor and Trustee Responsibilities

Executor: Also called a personal representative in some states, is responsible for managing an estate's financial affairs after someone dies, including probate procedures, tax filings, and asset distribution according to the will or living trust.

Trustee: A Person or Organization that helps Manage trust assets in the trust for the trust's beneficiaries, manages tax filings, and ensures assets are distributed per the trust terms. Unlike and executor, a trustee's responsibilities start when a trust is formed and can continue for years.

Key Points on Establishing a Living Trusts

Asset Transfer: Assets are transferred from your name to the trust's name, allowing you to maintain control as the trustee.

Control: You retain full control over assets in the trust as the trustee and can make changes as needed.

Asset Transfer Process: While transferring assets into a trust may take time, it consolidates all assets under one plan for protection. The time invested in forming a living trust with a qualified organization is worth the investment to protect all your assets and leave a legacy behind for your loved ones.

In summary, a living trust offers advantages over a will by avoiding probate, ensuring control during incapacity, and maintaining privacy. Executors and trustees play crucial roles in managing estates and trusts respectively, ensuring that assets are distributed according to the deceased's wishes.

True Story:

There was a grandma who was a widow she wanted to protect her assets and leave a family legacy. Grandma established a living trust with her attorney. Grandma had five grown children. When grandma passed away, her children gathered all her documents. The children never asked proper questions about her business affairs. In the discovery of managing her estate, they realized grandma's home was not properly transferred into the living trust. The estate went into probate. After five years of probate paying attorney and court fees the judge ruled in favor of the heirs. However, when the children sold the property all the monies from the sale of the home had to pay the probate and court fees. There was no inheritance left to distribute after paying legal fees. Let this be a lesson. Check your parents' property tax billing statement after a trust is formed. The billing statement should say i.e., Smith Family Living Trust. In this true story the property tax statement never said Trust, it only said grandma's name. This was a simple fix. Take the time to ask your parents questions, review paperwork and make certain all assets are transferred properly into the living trust.

Chapter 2: Preparing for the Role of Executor

Before stepping into the role of an executor, it is essential to undertake these key steps to ensure a smooth and efficient administration of the estate.

Steps to Take Before Becoming an Executor

1. Understand the Will or Living Trust: Familiarize yourself with the deceased's will or living trust to comprehend their wishes and how they want their assets distributed. Take time to discuss your parents' wishes while they are still alive to ensure a clear understanding of the living trust. Be realistic, one day your parents will be gone so cherish the time you have with them. Ask every question you can think of while they are able to answer i.e. What do want your funeral services to be like? what kind of flowers do you want at your funeral? What color casket do you want? What kind of music do you want us to play for you? What outfit do you want to wear for your funeral? What don't you want for your funeral services? Is there a Poem you want for your Program? Are there any items you wish to give away now before you pass away? How do you want me to manage the properties/assets? Ask questions to help make your job easier. I recommend recording your loved ones and creating a video testimony into an MP3 to play back one day to your siblings and have as a keepsake when you ask these questions. Lastly, ask your parents if all funeral arrangements are pre-paid, such as burial services, cremation, a mortuary. Ask for cemetery paperwork and mortuary information. Know if your parents have planned properly and if the funeral services are pre-paid or not. Plan for this expense if no arrangements are made. In most cases the opening and closing of burial plot is an extra cost, headstones, flowers, program printing and reception is not prepaid. Plan for these extra expenses.

2. Gather Important Documents: Collect essential documents such as the will, trust documents, financial statements, insurance policies, and contact information for beneficiaries and financial institutions. Check if your parents' home(s) is in the living trust, look at the yearly property tax billing statements. The Billing must list the property name under i.e., Smith Family trust. The Property Tax Bill must say family last name and the words Trust to ensure the property is transferred properly to your living trust. Plan while your parents are alive, make copies and or scan the living trust with all important documents, create a file, folder, binder, and store in a fireproof and waterproof safe box with all the vital documents. Do not wait until something happens. Practice the five P's: Proper Planning Prevents Poor Performance. If the property is not transferred properly into the living trust, contact your attorney immediately and fix it.

3. Notify Relevant Parties: Inform beneficiaries, financial institutions, creditors, and other relevant parties about the death and your role as executor. Death Certificates are required for notifying establishments i.e., Social Security, Medicare, Banks, Utility company (once you sell the property you then remove your parents' names from the utility billing, wait until the end for this step: you need utilities for a house inspection). Order 6-10 original death certificates depending how many relevant parties are listed in the trust. Not all establishments accept copies of the death certificate, majority want originals mailed. The official death certificate will be prepared by the funeral director, medical examiner, coroner, or certified physician. You will have to provide personal information about the deceased to expedite the process **such as: Full Name, Social Security Number, Last Known address, Marital Status, Last Known Occupation and Full Name of the Deceased's mother and father. Ask your parents for their parents (your grandparents maiden and married last names) write this down. Know this so you do not scramble.**

4. Secure Assets: Safeguard assets in a fire and waterproof safe box to prevent loss or damage, ensuring they are properly maintained until distribution. Depending on the scenario, if a home is vacant its best to have all locks changed to avoid any person having spare keys entering without your knowledge and taking valuable assets. Remove valuables from the home such as valuable Jewelry, heirlooms, anything that will be at risk of theft. Do not leave the house vacant if all possible. Leave a lamp with a timer operating nightly to appear as if the home is occupied at night. You may risk squatters inhabiting your deceased home if it appears abandoned. It is safe to have family or a person you trust reside in the deceased home until its sold or assets are distributed. Always think of the thief in the night lurking to steal. Lock and secure gates, windows, and doors. Asking trusted neighbors to keep an eye out on the property is advised. If all possible avoid announcing in the newspaper's obituary of a loved one's passing. I refused this option at the mortuary; you are announcing to thieves the home is vacant and identity theft can also take place. Keep your family's loss private. I have experienced criminals opening credit cards under the deceased name. This really happens. Thieves thrive when you are vulnerable.

5. Consult Professionals: Seek guidance from legal and financial professionals to navigate complex legal and tax requirements associated with estate administration. Depending on which state you live in and the quantity of assets, the process can take 2-5+ years to complete or longer if obstacles arise. During this process immediately file a claim for **Reassessment Exclusion** for **Transfer between Parent and child Prop 19 (formerly Prop 58 in California)**. Laws change in each state and Propositions are amended. Contact your local County Assessor's office, download correct forms for each state and file **(California BOE-19 and BOE266: Claim for Homeowner's Property Tax Exemption).** The new Prop 19 only excludes tax reassessment if an heir makes the property inherited as a primary resident as of February 26, 2021. Please Investigate this exclusion to avoid your current family property taxes from being reassessed. The reappraisal exclusion protects you if you have a living trust, inherited properties from your parents and you make the property a principal residence. The living trust protects you as an heir. Selling your parents' home can take years, avoid your property taxes from being reassessed. Hire an Estate Attorney to help you file all your exclusions correctly.

True Story: A family lost their last parent alive in the trust. It took two years to sell their parents' home. There were so much accumulated items. Finally, the home was ready to sell. The home sold as is and the heirs received the distribution of monies and were very happy to finally be done. However, the executor 4 months later received a reassessment tax bill from their local county assessor's office. The family never filed an exclusion for the transfer between parent and child form. The county took the last person who passed away date of death until the house sold. The reassessment taxes reflected the current market value of the home. Sadly, the executor did not leave emergency funds in the trust account and is responsible for paying this bill. The executor can try to collect monies from the heirs in hopes to pay for this mistake. The county assessor's office allows a grace period to file the exclusion. Contact your local county assessor's office to properly file this exclusion. Always, leave emergency money in the trust account for unforeseen trust expenses before you distribute all monetary inheritances. Don't be in a hurry to close out the account leave open one to two years after all business has been completed. Learn from this story.

Importance of Understanding the Terms of the Living Trust

- **Clarity on Distribution**: Understanding the terms of the living trust is crucial for ensuring estate assets are distributed according to the deceased's wishes without uncertainty or misinterpretation.

- **Compliance with Legal Requirements**: By comprehending the trust terms, you can ensure that all actions taken as an executor align with legal requirements and the trust's provisions.

- **Avoiding Disputes**: Clear understanding of the trust terms helps prevent conflicts among beneficiaries and ensures a smooth administration process. Making copies of the living trust for each sibling/heir is important to avoid conflict. Encourage the heirs to read the family living trust to ensure they are all clear on the terms. Resolve conflicts diplomatically by addressing disputes or conflicts among beneficiaries with empathy, patience, and a focus on finding amicable solutions that align with the trust's objectives. Be respectful, calm, professional, peaceful, kind and honor your parents' wishes. If all else fails, find a mediator to help facilitate your role.

In conclusion, thorough preparation before assuming the role of an executor is vital for effectively managing an estate. Understanding the terms of a living trust is particularly important as it guides asset distribution, ensures compliance with legal requirements, and minimizes potential disputes among beneficiaries. When in doubt align yourself with experts, hire estate consultants or living trust attorneys to help you navigate this process. Save and keep track of all receipts and paid invoices from the trust expenses. If the trust can afford these services, all expenses come out of the living trust monies. If your estate does not have liquid cash, you pay the expenses associated to the trust management. You get reimbursed when the sale of the property takes place, life insurance payouts, investment funds and or sale of assets. You may have to ask all your siblings to contribute for expenses, if they are able i.e., of expenses: hiring an attorney, paying property taxes, fumigating the home before selling the property, fixing leaks, roof repairs, termite repairs, unforeseen repairs of the home and more. Keep an excel sheet or ledger with entries of all expenses to track your expenditures of the estate expenses before you make distributions to heirs, these expenses are deducted before everything is finalized. You then reimburse yourself(s) and contributors for the out-of-pocket personal expenses made on behalf of the trust. Take those deductions from the trust monies as a refund, then distribute the inheritance monies to all beneficiaries after deductions are made. Again, if the Estate has liquid monies, you use the trust account to pay for all expenses. Important to keep a ledger, notebook with a list of expenses, excel sheet, receipts, invoices, and copies of all expenses. The role of an executor is to be transparent, honest, organized, and initiative-taking with the Estate administration duties. If asked to show proof of expenditures or family members falsely accusing you of fraud, you have documentation. Protect yourself and stay organized. Treat this as a business.

Chapter 3: Dealing with Grief and Family Dynamics

Coping with the loss of parents can be a deeply emotional and challenging experience, compounded by family dynamics and potential conflicts among siblings. Here are strategies to help navigate these tough times effectively.

Addressing Emotional Challenges after the Loss of Parents

1. Allow Yourself to Grieve: It is essential to acknowledge and process your emotions, allowing yourself to grieve in your way and time. Grieving is a personal journey that takes time. Be patient with yourself and allow yourself to heal at your own pace. Everyone grieves differently. Take it one day at a time.

2. Seek Support: Lean on friends, family, or a therapist for emotional support and guidance through the grieving process. Find resources online to help you cope with your grieving process.

3. Maintain Self-Care: Prioritize self-care activities such as exercise, healthy eating, and sufficient rest to support your emotional well-being. Stay hydrated, take vitamins, allow yourself to heal and stay healthy.

4. Create Traditions: Establish traditions to honor your loves one, i.e., parents' Sunday dinners as a family tradition and find comfort in shared memories. Keep your family members traditions alive by continuing their legacy and memory. Your parents are always with you, they taught you everything you know. Cook a special recipe or go to a destination you all visited together. Keep those family traditions alive.

5. Join Support Groups: Remember you are not alone. Reach out to support groups or online communities where you can connect with others who are also grieving.

6. Find Meaning in Your Loss: As you navigate through your grief, try to find meaning in the loss of your parents. This could involve reflecting on the lessons they taught you, the love they shared, or the legacy they left behind. Grieving the loss of parents is a complex process that requires patience, self-care, and support. By allowing yourself to grieve and seeking help when needed, you can gradually find healing and peace in honoring the memory of your parents.

Strategies for Handling Conflicts Among Siblings

1. Open Communication: Foster open and honest communication with siblings to address concerns, share feelings, and work towards resolving conflicts. Create a group text or email chat to keep everyone on the same page. Emails is an efficient way to keep a thread of all conversations.

2. Listen Actively: Practice active listening to understand each sibling's perspective without judgment or interruption. When conversations get heated or out of control, stop and regroup. Reschedule your meeting for another day to allow emotions and feelings to rest and settle. Do not judge. Be open to other suggestions and ideas. Do not take anything personal. Everyone is under stress and grieving.

3. Seek Mediation: If conflicts escalate that cannot be resolved among siblings, consider involving a neutral third party or mediator to facilitate constructive discussions and find common ground. Do not give up, find a third party immediately to help with the communication barriers or disagreements. This advice is critical to keeping your family glued together during this stressful, difficult, and emotional time.

4. Focus on Solutions: Collaborate with siblings to find practical solutions that prioritize the well-being of all family members involved. Everyone's input is valid, try to find a resolution together with peace and harmony. Remember, what would mom and dad want.

5. Set Boundaries: Establish clear boundaries and expectations to manage conflicts effectively and prevent misunderstandings. Your boundaries tell other people how they can treat you – what is acceptable and what is not. By addressing emotional challenges after the loss of parents and implementing strategies for handling conflicts among siblings, you can navigate these challenging times with resilience, compassion, and understanding. Remember that seeking support, maintaining open communication, and prioritizing self-care are key components of coping effectively with grief and family dynamics.

Setting Boundaries with Siblings as Executor of a Living Trust After the Loss of Parents

I cannot emphasize enough how important these steps below are to avoid conflicts. Managing a living trust as the executor while dealing with the loss of parents can be emotionally and logistically challenging, especially when navigating relationships with siblings. Here are some more tips on how to set boundaries effectively:

Communicate Clearly

Establish open and honest communication with your siblings from the beginning. Clearly outline your role as the executor and the responsibilities involved in managing the living trust. If you do not know the answer, find out before replying or answering. This is a learning process.

Define Roles and Responsibilities

Clearly define each sibling's role in the process to avoid misunderstandings or conflicts. Assign tasks based on individual strengths and availability. Not everyone is the same, however your parents chose you for a reason. They saw something in you, that they did not see with your other siblings. You can do this. Delegate as much as you can.

Set Expectations Early On

Discuss expectations regarding decision-making, financial matters, and communication. Establish boundaries from each sibling to ensure a smooth process. Delegating realistic tasks to each sibling's abilities helps you relieve stress. Create a to do list to check off tasks when completed. Stay organized and be efficient with your time. Trust the process.

Respect Each Other's Opinions

Acknowledge and respect each sibling's perspective and input. Encourage open dialogue while maintaining a respectful and understanding attitude towards differing opinions. The goal is to continue being siblings in harmony, peace, and love. Do not let this power get to your head. Maintain impartiality and make decisions based on the trust's guidelines rather than personal biases or pressures from beneficiaries. Pace yourself, think things through and then make decisions.

Prioritize Transparency

Keep all siblings informed about important decisions, updates, and financial matters related to the living trust. Transparency can help build trust and prevent misunderstandings. You will either experience unity or discord with your siblings. Keep positive and focus on how your parents would want you to behave with each other if they were alive. The goal is to honor your parents' wishes. Make them proud. You can do this.

Establish Boundaries for Communication

Set boundaries around communication by designating specific times or methods for discussing trust-related matters. This can help maintain focus and prevent constant interruptions. You will be stressed and overwhelmed. Be sure to take breaks and rest. Expect challenges along the way and be prepared to adapt to unforeseen circumstances with resilience and determination. It is okay to stop, breathe, and refocus.

Take Care of Yourself

Remember to prioritize self-care during this challenging time. Managing a living trust and dealing with the loss of parents can be emotionally draining, so make sure to take breaks, seek support, and practice self-care activities.

Seek Legal Advice

If you encounter complex legal issues or disagreements with siblings that you are unable to resolve independently, consider seeking legal advice from a professional specializing in estate planning or trust administration.

By setting clear boundaries, fostering open communication, and prioritizing transparency and respect, you can navigate the complexities of managing a living trust as an executor while maintaining positive relationships with your siblings during the grieving process. In a perfect world every family gets along and there are no problems. I would be lying to you if I said you will not have any issues. If you plan for the unexpected, you will not be surprised. Families fall apart after both parents pass away. My goal is for you to avoid the dismantling of your family. Focus on staying strong with your siblings, become glue and unbreakable, like mom and dad wanted.

Chapter 4: Managing Assets and Finances when both parents pass away.

Effectively managing assets and finances, especially in the context of estate planning and administration, requires careful diligence and collaboration with financial professionals and legal advisors. Here are steps to inventory assets and liabilities of an estate and guidance on collaborating with experts in the field.

Inventorying Assets and Liabilities of the Estate

1. Gather Documentation: Collect all relevant documents such as bank statements, investment accounts, real estate deeds, insurance policies, wills, trusts, and debts. Knowing your parents' assets and location of all documents while they are alive will help you navigate this task. Do not wait until your parents' pass to get organized, your job will be harder. Periodically ask your parents while they are alive for updated documents, passwords, or records. Keep a file, accordion folder or safe with documents.

2. List Assets: Compile a comprehensive list of assets including real estate, vehicles, bank accounts, investments, retirement accounts, private property, and business interests. Tip: Gather your parents' passwords to all online accounts, this helps tremendously. Proper Planning Prevents Poor Performance.

3. Assess Valuation: Determine the value of each asset to understand the estate's overall worth accurately. Appraise family heirlooms, jewelry or check online for the value. Strive to distribute assets equitably among beneficiaries, considering all heirs needs and the deceased's intentions.

4. Identify Liabilities: Document all debts and liabilities such as mortgages, loans, credit card balances, taxes owed, and outstanding bills. These debts must be paid by the trust monies or sale of home. Scenario, if your parents had no assets or property most credit card debt is forgiven if there was no co-signer to take responsibility. You have a Living trust; this means you have property and may need to pay any debts with the trust money and assets. Read each policies bylaws before calling the establishments. Know your rights and educate yourself on paying debts after your parents pass away.

Organize Information: Maintain a detailed inventory with clear descriptions, values, and ownership details for each asset and liability. Keep detailed records of all decisions made during estate administration to ensure transparency and accountability in asset distribution.

Collaborating with Financial Professionals and Legal Advisors

1. Consult a Financial Planner: Seek guidance from a financial planner to develop a comprehensive financial plan that aligns with your goals and ensures efficient management of assets.

2. Engage an Estate Planning Attorney: Work with an estate planning attorney to review legal documents and ensure compliance with relevant laws. When it comes to estate planning, enlisting the expertise of an estate planning attorney is crucial for ensuring your assets are protected and distributed according to your wishes.

3. Collaborate with an Accountant: Consult an accountant to address tax implications of asset transfers, assess potential tax liabilities, and optimize tax strategies for the estate.

4. Hire a Probate Lawyer: If probate is required, engage a probate lawyer to navigate the legal process efficiently and ensure proper distribution of assets according to the will or trust. You do not have to go through probate if your parents established a living trust properly. Ensure the property taxes says i.e., Smith Family Trust on the billing info. The property taxes must show the real estate property(s) is transferred into the trust by your local county recorder's office when the trust was created. This is a pro tip to confirm your estate attorney filed the paperwork correctly. This tip saves you money, headaches, probate and protects your family legacy.

True Story:

There was an executor who was very capable of managing all estate affairs. The executor met with two attorneys to review the trust and ensure everything was in order. The estate attorney wanted to charge $5000+ to manage the entire estate, appraise each asset with a fine-tooth comb. Instead, the executor felt the assets, can be distributed fairly among the siblings. A meeting took place in the parent's home and all the siblings took turns requesting items they wanted. This orderly process is possible if all siblings are amicable. When an attorney manages an estate, each item is appraised and given a value. The value of each item given to each heir is then added up as a distribution value amount and then deducted from the heir's inheritance. Example, Sibling one received a vintage car appraised at $10,000 then amount is deducted from the final inheritance distributed. The executor felt it was best to manage each asset individually and dispersed each item fairly per each sibling's request. There was no value deduction taken. The executor saved $5000. Everyone was happy and the estate saved money.

5. **Regular Review Meetings**: Schedule regular meetings with financial professionals and legal advisors to review asset performance, update estate plans as needed, and address any emerging financial or legal concerns.

By meticulously inventorying assets and liabilities of the estate and collaborating with experienced financial professionals and legal advisors, you can effectively manage assets and finances while ensuring compliance with legal requirements and optimizing financial outcomes for the estate. These services come with a price if you can afford it.

As mentioned before, if your parents can distribute any heirlooms, jewelry, or assets now while they are alive, this process makes your job easier. There might be a special item that is going to be desirable by a sibling, have your parents agree to distribute what they can while alive saves you trouble. Your parents will feel joy in gifting their precious heirlooms to family member while alive. Encourage purging and cleaning out clutter, clean the garage, donate unused items, donate old clothes, sorting and clean your parent's home will take months sometimes years depending on how much accumulated possessions are in the home or in a storage unit. Plan, think of the future job that lays ahead. If you can start cleaning out the junk now, do it. Do not wait for your parents to pass away. As your parents get older, it is a safety issue if you make their home safe to live in.

Additional Steps to Collaborate with Legal Experts for Comprehensive Planning if you need a Living Trust.

Assess Your Needs

Before meeting with an estate planning attorney, assess your financial situation, assets, and goals. Determine what you want to achieve through estate planning, such as asset protection, minimizing taxes, or providing for loved ones. A living trust protects you from costly probate fees.

Research and Select an Attorney

Research reputable estate planning attorneys in your area. Look for professionals with experience in estate planning, trust administration, and probate law. Consider referrals from trusted sources or professional organizations.

Schedule a Consultation

Contact the attorney's office to schedule an initial consultation. Use this meeting to discuss your goals, ask questions about their experience and approach to estate planning, and assess if they are a good fit for your needs.

Review Legal Documents

Work closely with your estate planning attorney to review existing legal documents such as wills, trusts, powers of attorney, and healthcare directives. Ensure these documents reflect your current wishes and are legally sound.

Immediately Establish a Living Trust if your parents do not have one.

If your parents are alive and need to protect their assets establish a living trust immediately. Depending on your financial situation and goals, your living trust attorney may recommend establishing trusts such as revocable living trusts, irrevocable trusts, or special needs trusts. Trusts can provide asset protection, privacy, and control over distribution. Get a living trust if you have property, assets, and investments. Protect your family legacy.

True Story:

There was a single mother who owned a home. Her daughter and her new husband lived with mom. Mom felt transferring her home into her daughter's name was a secure way to keep her legacy in the family. Mom did not know about a living trust. After six months, mom was no longer welcome in the home. The daughter legally owned the home and kicked out mom because she wanted her privacy. Lesson here, protect yourself and your assets. Get a living trust. Keep your home to live in until you pass away.

Ensure Compliance with Laws

Your estate planning attorney will guide you through the legal requirements and implications of estate planning decisions. They will ensure that your plan complies with relevant state and federal laws to avoid potential challenges in the future.

Regularly Review and Update Your Plan

Estate planning is not a one-time event; it requires periodic review and updates. Collaborate with your attorney to revisit your plan regularly, especially after major life events such as marriage, divorce, birth of children, or changes in financial circumstances.

Collaborate with Other Professionals

Your estate planning attorney may collaborate with other professionals such as financial advisors, accountants, or insurance agents to create a comprehensive plan that addresses all aspects of your financial well-being.

By following these steps and working closely with an experienced estate planning attorney, you can create a customized plan that protects your assets, provides for your loved ones, and ensures peace of mind knowing that your wishes will be executed according to the law.

Scenario, if one parent passes away and there was no living trust, but the home has both your parents name on it as tenants in common the living spouse is still able to keep the house and live in it. The problem is when the remaining parent passes away and there is no living trust you will go to probate. Immediately establish a living trust the first chance you get before any parent passes away or when the living parent is alive establish a trust, do not wait.

Chapter 5: Communication and Transparency

Clear communication with siblings and beneficiaries is crucial in estate planning and administration to foster trust, minimize conflicts, and ensure a smooth process. Maintaining transparency throughout the process is key to managing expectations and promoting understanding among all parties involved. Here are strategies to enhance communication and transparency in estate matters.

Importance of Clear Communication with Siblings and Beneficiaries

1. Building Trust: Transparent communication builds trust among siblings and beneficiaries, fostering a collaborative approach to estate matters.

2. Minimizing Conflicts: Clear communication helps prevent misunderstandings, reduce conflicts, and address concerns proactively.

3. Managing Expectations: Open dialogue sets realistic expectations regarding asset distribution, timelines, and responsibilities, avoiding surprises or disappointments.

4. Honoring Wishes: Communicating openly ensures that the deceased's wishes are understood and respected by all parties involved.

5. Strengthening Relationships: Effective communication can strengthen family relationships by promoting understanding, empathy, and cooperation during a challenging time.

Strategies for Maintaining Transparency Throughout the Process

1. Hold Family Meetings: Schedule regular family meetings to discuss estate plans, share updates on the administration process, and address any questions or concerns. Sunday dinners with family is a beautiful tradition. Rotate who will host Sunday dinners if you have siblings or pick a favorite restaurant. Keep your family tight.

2. Provide Regular Updates: Keep siblings and beneficiaries informed through regular updates via email, phone calls, or in-person meetings to ensure transparency.

3. Document Decisions: Maintain detailed records of decisions made during estate planning and administration to provide clarity on the rationale behind choices.

4. Encourage Questions: Create an open environment where siblings and beneficiaries feel comfortable asking questions and seeking clarification on estate matters.

5. Share Information Equally: Ensure equal access to information for all siblings and beneficiaries to promote fairness and transparency in the decision-making process.

By prioritizing clear communication with siblings and beneficiaries and implementing strategies for maintaining transparency throughout the estate planning and administration process, you can foster positive relationships, mitigate conflicts, and ensure a harmonious journey towards fulfilling the deceased's wishes with understanding and cooperation. Make your parents proud. Keep your family together during this challenging time.

True Story:

There was an executor who had unpredictable siblings. The executor had to solely manage all the affairs of the estate. Unfortunately, the siblings went behind the executors back and took assets from the home without informing the executor. Every sibling had a house key and gained access to the home. During the home cleaning process, appliances, furniture, heirlooms, and personal items disappeared with no communication. The executor immediately changed the locks to the home. The siblings were angry about the lock change and turned against the executor. The executor became the bad guy in this story for trying to preserve order. The entire process was a discord, stressful, unmanageable, and emotionally unhealthy. The lesson here is, change the locks immediately. Save yourself stress. Avoid this problem when dealing with entitled and greedy siblings. You will learn a lot about a person when an inheritance is involved.

Chapter 6: Resolving Disputes and Handling Greed

In estate planning and administration, identifying signs of greed among siblings and implementing techniques to resolve conflicts are essential for maintaining harmony and fairness in the distribution of assets. Here are strategies to recognize greed and effectively address disputes within the family.

Identifying Signs of Greed Among Siblings

1. Unequal Demands: Siblings showing a powerful desire for a disproportionate share of assets or benefits may indicate greed. It happens in every family. You are not exempt from this behavior.

2. Lack of Transparency: Individuals withholding information or being secretive about financial matters could signal selfish motives. Approach the individual with other siblings to have witnesses of the conversation. Do not underestimate the person with whom you are dealing.

3. Resistance to Compromise: Unwillingness to negotiate or consider others' perspectives may suggest a self-centered approach driven by greed. You will deal with multiple personalities and behaviors.

4. Manipulative Behavior: Attempts to influence decisions solely for personal gain rather than the family's best interests can be a sign of greed. Stand your ground, follow the trust.

Disregard for Fairness: Ignoring the deceased's wishes or disregarding equitable distribution principles in favor of personal gain may indicate greed. Continue to express your parents' wishes.

Techniques for Resolving Conflicts and Preventing Disputes

1. Facilitate Open Dialogue: Encourage honest and respectful communication among siblings to address concerns, clarify intentions, and find common ground. Creating a group chat via text for casual communication and email for formal decisions and keeping an email thread for records of conversations.

2. Seek Mediation: Engage a neutral third party, such as a mediator or counselor, to facilitate discussions, promote understanding, and guide conflict resolution.

3. **Establish Clear Guidelines**: Define clear rules and guidelines for asset distribution in advance to prevent misunderstandings and reduce the potential for disputes.

4. **Focus on Fairness**: Emphasize fairness and equity in decision-making processes to ensure that each sibling's interests are considered.

5. **Consider Professional Advice**: Consult with financial advisors, legal experts, or estate planners to provide objective guidance on asset distribution and conflict resolution strategies.

By proactively identifying signs of greed among siblings, promoting open communication, and implementing conflict resolution techniques focused on fairness and collaboration, families can navigate estate disputes effectively while upholding the deceased's wishes with integrity and respect. Prioritizing transparency, empathy, and constructive dialogue can help prevent conflicts from escalating and foster a harmonious resolution for all parties involved.

True Story:

There was a mom and dad who formed a living trust to leave their children a legacy. They chose one child to be the executor. The oldest sibling was a single mom and lived with mom and dad. The oldest daughter tried to convince mom and dad to transfer the home under her name. The daughter was using scare tactics to convince mom and dad to quick claim deed the home to her and their granddaughter who lived with mom and dad. Luckily, the executor was initiative-taking with mom and dad. The executor always communicated to mom and dad about never signing any documents without the presence of the executor and or an attorney. Mom felt pressured and uneasy about the daughter's action and tactics. Mom called the executor to explain what was going on with the sibling who resided with mom and dad. Immediately the executor stopped the action and made it noticeably clear that the living trust was to protect mom and dad's assets and their home. There was no need to transfer the home to the daughter. The lesson here is the daughter was greedy, entitled and was taking possession of the home to eliminate the other siblings from an inheritance. Always inform your parents to never sign documents without the executor's knowledge. Trust is very essential in choosing an executor.

Chapter 7: Legal Considerations and Compliance in Estate Administration

In estate planning and administration, understanding the legal requirements and ensuring compliance with tax laws and regulations are critical aspects of managing an estate effectively. Here is an overview of the legal considerations for estate administration and strategies to maintain compliance with relevant laws.

Overview of Legal Requirements for Estate Administration

Gathering Assets: The estate administration process involves collecting the deceased's assets, paying debts, filing tax returns, and distributing remaining assets to beneficiaries.

State Laws: Variability across states estate administration laws vary from state to state, influencing how assets are distributed, wills are validated, and debts are settled after an individual's death.

Executor Appointment: A last will nominates an executor to oversee estate administration; if no will exist, anyone can request to serve as the estate's executor or administrator.

Real Estate Transfer: Real estate property transfer is governed by state law, typically administered in the state where the decedent resided at death.

Estate Planning: Comprehensive estate planning involves creating legal documents like wills, living trusts, powers of attorney, and advanced health care directives.

Ensuring Compliance with Tax Laws and Regulations

Tax Compliance: Estate administrators must comply with tax laws by filing necessary tax returns and addressing potential tax liabilities associated with asset transfers.

Legal Advice: Seeking guidance from financial advisors, legal experts, or estate planners can help ensure compliance with tax laws and optimize tax strategies for the estate.

Regular Updates: Keeping abreast of changes in tax laws and regulations is essential to maintain compliance throughout the estate administration process.

By understanding the legal requirements for estate administration, ensuring compliance with tax laws and regulations, seeking professional advice when needed, and staying informed about legal updates, individuals can effectively manage estates while adhering to legal standards and fulfilling their responsibilities as executors or administrators. Prioritizing legal considerations and compliance is crucial for a smooth and legally sound estate administration process. You are not alone you have online resources, services, and experts you can align yourself with to execute this job. No one prepares enough for this role. I hope to guide you through the toughest job you will ever have. You chose to read this book for a reason. Continue to seek answers, learn as much as you can about being an executor. Your parents chose you to make them proud. Keep your eye on the prize. Finish strong.

True Story:

Mom and dad had a family living trust. There are three siblings, and one was the executor. Dad passed away and mom needed a caregiver. Mom still lived in her home and one sibling moved in to take care of mom. The executor did not live close by. The sibling who became the caregiver took mom to the attorney one day unbeknownst to the executor and had the living trust changed. Executor #1 was removed from the trust and the sibling (caregiver) was now the new executor #2. The sibling convinced mom to go along with the change. When executor #1 tried to log into mom's banking account to pay bills, access was denied to the account. Immediately executor #1 went to mom's house to ask questions and executor #2 stopped executor #1 at the front door. The sibling explained mom did not trust executor #1 anymore and changed the living trust. Executor #1 was prohibited from speaking to mom. Executor #2 then falsely accused executor #1 of embezzling money. Executor #1 then received a letter from mom's attorney stating executor #1 was being sued for embezzling money. Executor #1 was in disbelief of the false accusations. The lesson of this story is to be careful who you entrust with your parents. Be in communication with your attorney about siblings' bad intentions. Executor #2 convinced mom she was being taken advantage of by executor #1. Be watchful and learn from this story. If you can care for your parents take on that role and hire honest caregivers to help you. Avoid this horrific story of greed. The sibling's intentions were to keep the home and not have to share the inheritance.

Chapter 8: Distribution of Assets and Closing the Estate

1. Managing the distribution of assets: According to a living trust and completing the estate administration process involves crucial steps. Understanding these processes is essential for executors to fulfill their duties effectively. Here is a detailed guide on distributing assets, closing the estate, and key points in managing a family estate as an executor.

2. Steps Involved in Distributing Assets According to the Living Trust: Begin by compiling an inventory of all assets held in the living trust, including real estate, financial accounts, private property, and investments.

3. Debt Settlement: Prioritize settling any outstanding debts and liabilities of the deceased using estate funds before distributing assets to beneficiaries. Keep the bank trust accounts open until all debt in the estate and bills have been paid. Do not close the trust account until all monies have been distributed especially after a sale of the family home(s) you need a bank account to send escrow money to. Keeping your parents bank account open for living trust business allows you to separate the expenses from yours. You will need a death certificate to show the bank proof of parents passing and copy of the trust to become the administrator. Speak to the bank branch manager they will walk you through the process of adding you to the trust account.

4. Following Trust Instructions: Adhere to the instructions outlined in the living trust document regarding asset distribution among beneficiaries.

5. Specific Gifts: Distribute specific gifts mentioned in the trust first, followed by the remaining assets according to the trust's provisions. If you have unlisted items in the estate that heirs are requesting, divide the assets among the siblings as fairly as you can. Take turns picking items and ask who wants what item. Any unwanted items can be donated, sold, or discarded. Certain assets may hold a sentimental value to one sibling and a different meaning to another sibling. Try your best to be fair and considerate.

6. When a Living Trust is Funded: After the owners pass away a trust is considered funded when the assets specified in the trust document are successfully transferred into the trust's name following the death of the grantors. This process involves re-titling ownership of assets, such as real estate, investments, bank accounts, and private property, into the trust's name to ensure they are managed and distributed according to the terms outlined in the trust document. Upon the death of the grantors, the successor trustee takes over the management of the trust and oversees the funding process. Assets outside the trust that were not previously transferred into the trust during the grantors' lifetime may need to go through probate if their ownership is not clearly designated in the trust document.

However, if the grantors clearly intended for these assets to be part of the trust but failed to transfer them before passing away, legal mechanisms like Heggstad petitions can sometimes be used in some states to include these assets in the trust without going through probate. A trust is funded after the owners pass away when all intended assets are properly titled in the name of the trust, allowing for efficient administration and distribution of assets to beneficiaries as per the grantors' wishes. Align yourself with experts during this process. You will be fine, follow the steps and guide to help you navigate this journey.

7. Asset Transfer: Transfer assets to beneficiaries as per the trust's guidelines, ensuring compliance with legal requirements and tax implications. Allow for unexpected expenses, unforeseen attorney fees, taxes that may arise for the estate. Leave a portion of money in the bank account before you close out everything i.e., the estate is worth $800,000 after debts are paid and distribution to heirs were made, leave $2,000 - $5,000 in the trust bank account to use for an emergency or unforeseen expenses that may arise for six months to a one year after you make all distributions. When all is in the clear and there are no expenses, then you distribute the remaining balance of the account to all heirs. I speak from experience. You may have to pay taxes on the estate, pay a debt you did not know about or a medical bill you did not know your parents had. The estate must file its own separate taxes. Every heir/beneficiary is responsible for filing their own personal taxes after the distribution of the inheritance.

Closing Procedures for Completing the Estate Administration Process

Final Distribution: Once all estate assets are gathered, debts settled, and taxes filed, initiate the final distribution of assets to beneficiaries as outlined in the trust document. I.e., if you are selling a family home, and there's liquid cash in the bank accounts wait for the sale of the home to close with escrow before you distribute monies. When selling a home there are expenses such as termite tenting, repairs, code violations, and more come out of the trust. The executor is responsible for managing the monies of the estate during these transactions. Do not rush to empty the bank accounts. You will need money to pay for expenses that arise. I.e., if you have a sibling that is struggling financially and in dire need of a cash advancement, you can make a reasonable advancement distribution taken from their inheritance amount. Create a contract for them to sign and agree to deduct the advancement at the time of the final distribution of monies. All heirs must agree of this distribution. Hardship exists and families are all on various levels of income.

Court Approval: Obtain court approval for asset distribution if required by probate laws or if probate was part of the estate administration process. Let us hope you do not go through probate because you have a living trust and your parents planned properly.

Executor Duties: As an executor or successor trustee, ensure that all legal and financial obligations are met before closing the estate. Double check all your work.

Estate Closure: Finalize all administrative tasks, including transferring remaining assets, settling disputes, and obtaining court approval if you go through probate for closing the estate. You are at the finish line. You did an excellent job. Pat yourself on the back. You are an expert and can help others with this process. Pay it forward and share your knowledge. Continue to honor your parents and keep your family legacy alive. You have a lot to be proud of.

Recap of Key Points in Managing a Family Estate as an Executor

- **Legal Compliance:** Ensure compliance with state laws, tax regulations, and trust provisions throughout the estate administration process.

- **Communication:** Maintain open communication with beneficiaries to manage expectations and address concerns promptly.

- **Asset Management:** Handle asset distribution carefully, following trust instructions and prioritizing debt settlement.

- **Professional Guidance:** Seek advice from legal experts or financial advisors when navigating complex legal processes or tax matters.

Encouragement for Executors Facing Challenges with Greedy Siblings

Executors facing challenges with greedy siblings should prioritize fairness, transparency, and open communication. Seeking mediation or legal assistance can help resolve disputes effectively while upholding the deceased's wishes with integrity. By following these steps diligently, executors can successfully navigate asset distribution according to a living trust, complete the estate administration process efficiently, and manage family estates responsibly as entrusted executors.

I hope you find confidence, courage, peace, and comfort that you are not alone in this process. Sadly, families end up in turmoil and fall apart after the parents pass away. Keep focused on being the glue to keep your family together and in harmony. I hope these tips help you in your journey. I wish you the best of luck!

True Stories:

There were four siblings, mom and dad chose the youngest sibling as the executor. All the three other siblings got so jealous and turned against the executor. Mom and dad saw something in the youngest child that they did not see in the other children. The executor experience turmoil with the siblings. The executor got sick from the stress. The executor tried everything, however there was no reasoning with the siblings. It was a nightmare. These siblings are no longer speaking over who mom and dad chose as an executor, pure jealousy. Watch your back.

There were five siblings, mom and dad chose the eldest sibling to be executor. The executor was the caregiver for mom and dad until the end. The executor was exhausted. The other siblings were trying to remove the executor to make decisions claiming she had dementia and was unfit. This was not true only to create stress, difficulties, and manipulation during the estate process. The estate eventually became final. The executor became an outsider with her siblings. Trust was broken and the sibling's relationship is not the same as before.

There were three siblings, mom and dad chose the middle child to be the executor. Mom and dad were successful and well off. The executor helped run the family businesses and was remarkably close to his parents. The other two siblings did not come around to visit or took time to check on mom and dad. The executor cared for mom and dad's affairs and needs. Mom and dad passed away and the executor discovered his parents changed the living trust without him knowing. All the assets and monies would only go to the executor and not the other siblings. Mom and dad felt the other two siblings did not care about them. The two siblings were angry over the exclusion, felt entitled, and lawyered up to fight for and inheritance. The siblings had no chance, the trust was specific and clear. The executor carried mom and dad's wishes and the siblings no longer speak or have a relationship with the executor. The lesson here is, take loving care of your parents, because they took care of you. Do not take your parents for granted.

www.ingramcontent.com/pod-product-compliance
Lightning Source LLC
Chambersburg PA
CBHW031600210526
45464CB00003B/1359